snapshot·picture·library

FARM
ANIMALS

snapshot · picture · library

FARM ANIMALS

FOG CITY PRESS

Published by Fog City Press,
a division of Weldon Owen Inc.
415 Jackson Street
San Francisco, CA 94111 USA
www.weldonowen.com

WELDON OWEN INC.
Group Publisher, Bonnier Publishing Group John Owen
Chief Executive Officer and President Terry Newell
Senior Vice President, International Sales Stuart Laurence
Vice President, Sales and New Business Development Amy Kaneko
Vice President, Publisher Roger Shaw
Vice President, Creative Director Gaye Allen
Managing Editor, Fog City Press Karen Perez
Assistant Editor Sonia Vallabh
Art Director Kelly Booth
Designer Andreas Schueller
Design Assistant Justin Hallman
Production Director Chris Hemesath
Production Manager Michelle Duggan
Sales Manager Emily Bartle
Color Manager Teri Bell

Text Thomas Downs
Picture Research Brandi Valenza

A WELDON OWEN PRODUCTION
© 2007 Weldon Owen Inc.

Library of Congress Control Number: 2007936044

ISBN-13: 978-1-74089-990-1

10 9 8 7 6 5 4 3 2 1
2009   2010   2011 2012

Printed by Tien Wah Press in Singapore.

If you visit a farm, you are
sure to meet a lot of animals.
But you never know who
you'll run into until you get
there—every farm is different!

You could meet anything from a
chicken to a llama to a buffalo—
and maybe even this little lamb.

A lamb is a young sheep. Lambs sleep a lot, and they nibble on grass and weeds.

Baby lambs feel safer with their parents. So do baby birds, and baby pigs. Just like baby people!

Piglets are
usually born
in a group,
or litter, of
between six and
twelve babies.

A piglet loves to smear himself with mud by rolling in it. It's his way of keeping cool on hot days!

These little bunnies have
great big ears. They listen
hard to learn about the world.

Donkeys have big ears, too! Their call is a loud "hee-haw." Even when they are far apart, they can hear each other calling.

With some kinds of cows, both the males and females have horns. Other kinds of cows don't have horns at all.

These cows
can take naps
standing up,
although they
like to lie down
to get a good
deep sleep.

But while they're awake, these oxen are busy! Oxen are very strong bulls who are trained to pull wagons and plows.

These buffalo
are pretty big!
Adult male buffalo
can weigh as much
as a small car.

And speaking of big, the ostrich is the largest type of bird. Ostriches can't fly, but they can run faster than a person can!

These farm birds may not be as big as the ostrich, but they make up for it with their bright colors and showy feathers.

Roosters and chickens have showy colors too—red combs on their heads and bright red wattles below their beaks.

Other birds, such as this goose
and peacock, are white.

And then there are ducks and geese! These little birds are very good at swimming as well as flying.

This duck and this horse are exploring the farm in their own separate ways—down low and up high!

A baby horse is called a foal. Even though it can walk when it is only two hours old, a foal will keep close by its mother when exploring the farm.

Most horses
are used
for trail rides.
Some horses
are ridden
by farmers
who herd cattle
or sheep.

Horses of all ages need plenty of space to roam and graze. And plenty of space to exercise, run, and frolic!

Fences help to keep curious animals from wandering too far away and getting lost.

Watch out for goats! They are
so smart that they can open a gate
if the latch is within their reach.

Some goats have long hairs, like beards, below their chins. Usually bearded goats are males—but not always!

Alpacas are mostly
friendly, but when
they get mad,
they spit at each
other! They are
farmed for their
very soft wool.

Llamas are farmed for their wool and used to help carry heavy supplies. When llamas get very old their front teeth stick out.

Sheep also have useful wool. And as they get older their horns can get curlier and curlier!

Sheep tend to
hang out together.
A group of sheep
is called a flock.

Animals can form all sorts of friendships on the farm... like this cat and this duckling!

They might even like to
be friends with you!

Acknowledgments

Weldon Owen would like to thank the following people for their assistance in the production of this book: Diana Heom, Ashley Martinez, Danielle Parker, Lucie Parker, Phil Paulick, and Erin Zaunbrecher.